THE

OF THE

# MODERN
# WARRIOR

Books in Print

*Musashi's Book of Five Rings*
*Sun Tzu's Art of War*
*The Shogun's Scroll*
*Sword in the Boardroom*
*Zen and the Art of Stickfighting*
*Self-Revealization Acceptance – An Introduction*
*Practicing Self-Revealization Acceptance*
*The Lady of the Rings*
*Wit and Wisdom of an American Hanshi*
*The Hanshi of Central Park*
*The Hanshi in Brussels*
*Portraits of the Living Tao*
Coming Soon
*Cherry Blossoms for Children*
*Mastering Okinawan Sai*
*Hanshi's Guide to Ultimate Self-defense*
*Taikido - Life Force Energy Healing Exercises*
*Collected Poetry and Short Stories*
*Napoleon's Maxims for Business and War*

# THE WAY OF THE

## OF THE

# MODERN
# WARRIOR

*Living the Samurai Ideal
in the 21st Century*

**Stephen F. Kaufman**
Hanshi, Hebi-Ryu Karate

**TUTTLE** Publishing
Tokyo | Rutland, Vermont | Singapore

## The Tuttle Story: "Books to Span the East and West"

Most people are very surprised to learn that the world's largest publisher of books on Asia had its humble beginnings in the tiny American state of Vermont. The company's founder, Charles E. Tuttle, belonged to a New England family steeped in publishing. And his first love was naturally books—especially old and rare editions.

Immediately after WW II, serving in Tokyo under General Douglas MacArthur, Tuttle was tasked with reviving the Japanese publishing industry. He later founded the Charles E. Tuttle Publishing Company, which thrives today as one of the world's leading independent publishers.

Though a westerner, Tuttle was hugely instrumental in bringing a knowledge of Japan and Asia to a world hungry for information about the East. By the time of his death in 1993, Tuttle had published over 6,000 books on Asian culture, history and art—a legacy honored by the Japanese emperor with the "Order of the Sacred Treasure," the highest tribute Japan can bestow upon a non-Japanese.

With a backlist of 1,500 titles, Tuttle Publishing is more active today than at any time in its past—inspired by Charles Tuttle's core mission to publish fine books to span the East and West and provide a greater understanding of each.

Published by Tuttle Publishing, an imprint of Periplus Editions (HK) Ltd.

www.tuttlepublishing.com

Copyright © 2012 Stephen F. Kaufman

**Library of Congress Cataloging-in-Publication Data**

Kaufman, Steve, 1939-
The way of the modern warrior : living the samurai ideal in the 21st
century / Stephen F. Kaufman.
    p. cm.
ISBN 978-4-8053-1197-4 (pbk.)
1. Martial arts--Philosophy. 2. Samurai. I. Title.
GV1101.K34 2012
796.801--dc23

2012020651

ISBN 978-4-8053-1197-4

**Distributed by**

**North America, Latin America & Europe**
Tuttle Publishing
364 Innovation Drive
North Clarendon
VT 05759-9436 U.S.A.
Tel: 1 (802) 773-8930
Fax: 1 (802) 773-6993
info@tuttlepublishing.com
www.tuttlepublishing.com

**Asia Pacific**
Berkeley Books Pte. Ltd.
61 Tai Seng Avenue #02-12
Singapore 534167
Tel: (65) 6280-1330
Fax: (65) 6280-6290
inquiries@periplus.com.sg
www.periplus.com

**Japan**
Tuttle Publishing
Yaekari Building, 3rd Floor
5-4-12 Osaki, Shinagawa-ku
Tokyo 141 0032
Tel: (81) 3 5437-0171
Fax: (81) 3 5437-0755
sales@tuttle.co.jp
www.tuttle.co.jp

15 14 13 12    5 4 3 2 1    1209MP

Printed in Singapore

# *Contents*

INTRODUCTION

# The Samurai Ideal and the New Samurai

What does it actually mean to be a samurai and to maintain the attendant *bushido*, "way of the warrior," mentality? It is certainly not an easy discipline. If it were easy, then it would have no value and could easily be obtained with a Ph.D. But to be a samurai is not an intellectual pursuit. It is to live a certain life, one of morality, courage, and integrity, that offers great rewards that are generally not sought for in life. Along with this discipline comes incredible frustration and humility (among other things) before one can truly understand the self in relation to the ideal. Even when one is born into it there will be some attendant frustration.

Bushido did not come about by accident. Bushido is not a quaint notion about being a warrior and accomplishing warrior-like feats. It is the most intense personal discipline one can imagine. Why? It is because the idea of life and death as equal has to overcome the limitations of the intellect through the practice of an ideal. The samurai ideal is contemplative towards the finality of a situation or physical death. Most people confuse the attitude of death with the extinguishing of life, and in this they are confused. The idea is not to die in vain. Enlightened people, samurai or not, prefer dying to be meaningful and purposeful. Yes there is the formality of physical death, but there are many other forms of "death" that occur in a person's life. The death of an old way of thinking may be a more rational approach to the samurai ideal.

Bushido is usually associated with martial practice, and rightly so. The bushido aspect is relevant only because it denotes physical confrontation and mortal combat. That's all it is. It is in the application of military tactics and martial "arts" that the practitioner comes to understand the meaning of life through death and the meaning of death through life. This highly philosophical connection should not be confused with the intellectual pursuit of spiritual understanding. Spirit has nothing to do with it in the ordinary sense of the word. The ideal is mostly relegated to the application of one's personal endeavor and intention to be clear in mind and soul while at harmony with the entire universe. When one is clear in mind and soul, it is then unnecessary to dwell on the spiritual aspect of "being," because once understood, the practitioner is the spirit of the thing itself. One does not practice an "art" to attain spirituality. One becomes spiritual when the realization of the active pursuit of perfection is understood as foolish and meaningless. More of this will be explained as you venture deeper into this book.

Samurai means "to serve." Ah, but to serve what? We begin to move into the depths of understanding by asking the correct question, and when you do, the answer will always be found to be lying within the question itself. To serve what? The answer is always personal and usually meaningless to anyone else. For example, I may think that understanding the nature of mashed potatoes and the variations of perfection derived from that discipline would free me to be spiritually harmonious with the rest of the universe. And that is exactly right! It may not be what you have thought as a valid reason for existence, but whose existence are we talking about? A Potato Master's existence, not yours. The concept can, and does, include service to one's benefactor, or one's lord, if you will, the reason being is to maintain one's sustenance by providing what the lord requires. In return, I am fed, clothed, and housed. Do we detect some sort of trade off here? Absolutely! Service to a lord can include devotional practice to an ideal. The reality of bushido is such.

If one is willing to live an abstruse life and is willing to suffer the humiliation of starvation and living in a refrigerator carton due to a lack of understanding one's relationship to the universe, then go ahead and do that. I prefer the elegance of personal experience. In reality, not every samurai was a sword-wielding soldier. Not every soldier was a samurai. It was a class of people who attained that particular rank due to the evolution of the society as a whole. As a result, the samurai became elitist. Some samurai were administrators, some poets, artisans, priests, etc, with the exception of merchants. Merchants were considered parasites and unable to create or produce anything of meritorious value. It made no difference to the samurai that they, the merchants, controlled the country and the economy; they would have been unable to do so without the assistance of the samurai to protect their assets. Without soldiers to defend the realm, nothing else could exist, except in a state of perpetual bliss, which simply cannot exist.

Hence, disrespect existed between the merchant and warrior classes. Farmers and artisans; artisans and merchants, and so on, had the same issues between themselves. This class distinction had to be overcome by the High Regency in order for the country to become of value in the world community. In 1875, the wearing of swords was banned, but the samurai mentality was not. Those who endeavored to maintain the glorious history of a profound culture covertly adhered to the samurai ideal. However, many other samurai, and the samurai pretenders who never made it, immediately succumbed to the new rules of order, throwing the classes into chaos and anarchy.

One does not have to be a genius to realize what a civil war will do to a society. Any form of civil war is devastating to a culture. The results are obvious, and it takes a long time for the culture to reorganize itself as a functioning unit. Curiously, the merchant classes and other interested in wealth and power relegated the samurai ideal to the toilet. Nonetheless, the samurai principle and the attendant bushido mentality is what enabled the restructuring of the society as a whole, especially after World War II.

Be careful when you try to determine what "samurai" actually means. Your service to your self is "samurai." Your service to your sword is "samurai." Your service to your family is "samurai." Your service to your country is "samurai." Your service to your individual discipline is "samurai." Samurai is a universal concept. It can no longer be regarded as a simplistic Japanese cultural "thing."

Anyone who creates and maintains any higher ideal in and of his or her own self may be considered a samurai. A samurai, male or female, devotes their life to a perfection of their own higher self and does so for the benefit of all concerned, with themselves as the progenitor of the ideal, whether they are conscious of it or not. In order to attain higher levels of personal perfection, it is essential that the ideal incorporates the needs of humanity, but only if their personal view does not cloud their vision. Therefore, Mahatma Gandhi was samurai, Alexander the Great was samurai, Miles Davis was samurai, Betty Friedan was samurai, and even Salvador Dali was samurai. General George Patton was samurai. Getting the picture? It is all based on a specific discipline that overrides any cultural imitations and limitations that can readily be expressed in any arena of accomplishment. I focus my life towards a higher understanding of myself and to my arts while constantly maintaining the integrity of my work. Therefore, I am samurai.

This book is an exposition expounding the philosophy that maintained the structure of Japanese society for nearly one thousand years. Irrespective of the fact that, in the late eighteen hundreds, the leadership of Japan sought to quell the ideal of "service" in an attempt to modernize itself with regards to the rest of the world, especially the Western mentality.

With true understanding and a not-so-humble approach, I present these ideas to all men. These teachings, so vital to the existence of any culture's very life, can be and must be presented in an easily understood format that reflects on the current state of personal conduct and world affairs. It is not limited by geographic, religious, or political thought and policy, or gender identification. I have written this book so it is free from the allegory that usually accompanies works of this genre. Allegory does nothing more than present ideas that may only be naïve representations, thereby leaving the reader to wonder about the alleged profound implication of what is being transmitted. By the nature of their essence, unable to be clearly explained, the explanations therefore become meaningless.

In this book, I present realistic viewpoints of what is actually meant by other works that present "hidden" wisdom generally available only to the so-called initiated few. This *Hanshi Damashi*, or "Hanshi's Soul," is based on applications to life that transcend specific cultural implications relevant to only a small segment of the global community. It fits everyone, everywhere, and is applicable to every ideal. I use idealistic samurai principles and illustrate them with appropriate ideas that can be used to raise an individual's consciousness. For ease of reference and discussion by readers, they are presented numerically though in no particular order.

This book is not written as simple entertainment, nor is it an attempt to present simple tidbits of wisdom. It is a contemporary account of the manner in which people must conduct themselves if they would desire to be at peace with the world and themselves while maintaining harmony with the universe. Nor is it a religious book with rules and instructions for carrying out life's challenges. Fundamentally, it is a book of wisdom that everyone everywhere has at one time or another contemplated. From my own perspective, it is a serious endeavor to impart wisdom that is required for sane and practical living in today's societies. The examples I use do not run on and on with literary grace. They are to the point and are not to be read through as one would a novel.

Consider the implications of all examples and think about them. Accept those you feel are appropriate to your lifestyle, and disregard the rest until you are ready for further personal illumination. And always remember to place no value on things of no value—such as words of wisdom.

—*Hanshi Stephen F. Kaufman, New York, 2011*

# 1

## *Do Not Be Afraid of Change; It is the Only Thing That's Dependable*

Change occurs through all things at all times. Change is also known as life declaring its desire for new understanding and expression. If this did not occur then imminent death would be the result albeit not necessarily a physical death. When feelings of uncertainty arise in you it is usually the beginning of a new sense of consciousness even if you are resistant to the driving force that is creating the unrest and causing a desire for change. There is never progress without conflict. Even in the midst of understanding your chosen art at a new level of awareness, the old forms will create impediments and discomfort toward acceptance of the new because of their own sense of conceptual beingness relative to undergoing the prelude to change. When the desire for a different set of circumstances arises within you, it is essential that you consider the move to the new consciousness. It is your soul telling you it is time to move on. It will possibly reappear in your mind time after time until you make a decision. Eventually, if you don't, the feelings will subside and you may wonder later on why you didn't take advantage of your intuition. If you do, get ready for combat on any level from which it appears to emanate. Change in itself is not a bad thing if you are prepared and self-assured.

# 2

## *Think Well of Yourself and Let That Be Your Answer*

How you present yourself to the world is all-important and it indicates your self-worth. It should not be used however, with the intention of impressing others, because this is based on their lack of self-esteem and general inability to come to terms with themselves. If you concern yourself with the thoughts of others before you concern yourself with thoughts of yourself you will give others cause to criticize and judge you and your actions, which they will do anyway based on their own consternation. When handled adroitly, you will control the situation. On the other hand, when you become enamored of yourself, you will be sure to make errors and enemies. This happens because you are thinking about what others may be thinking about you and, when left unchecked, eventually creates interpersonal conflict that can lead to war. Thinking well of yourself includes the development of your skills in and through any art form or discipline you practice, or life-style you pursue. It is essential that you maintain the integrity of your own being first before attempting to influence others about their own integrity. If you do not think in the same way as the samurai, that is, to be of service to any and all concerned by maintaining your own vision, then you are worthless to yourself as well because you are not in harmony with yourself.

# 3

## *No One is Responsible for Your Fallacies—Probably Not Even Yourself*

We are all subject to the vagaries of life and the difficulties we must endure in everyday activities. How simpler things would be if we would only focus on one specific ideal—even if it eventually appears in our minds as a wrong choice. Wrong choices are part of the growing process of self-evolution and are necessary. If we learn from these errors in judgment and proceed they will aid us in reestablishing our prime condition. This takes guts. We are always ensnared by external entrapments: earning a livelihood, trying to provide for our families, being good to others. The list is endless. It would all fall into place if we would concern ourselves only with those things that can enhance our lives for the betterment of our own personal existence. Many of the de-

tours in life happen because of matters that are be-
yond our control. It is how you deal with adversity
that empowers you to move forward as the prime
recipient of your own ultimate good. When you are
good to yourself you will find no difficulty in being
good to others. But, you must come first. When you
come to understand the reasons for your actions, you
will readily see that decisions may or may not be necessary at that juncture.

# 4

## *It is Better to Take the Easy Way In Rather Than the Easy Way Out*

When you are confident in your endeavors, even though they may not be at a level of mastery, the road to mastery itself becomes easier to attain. When you have to struggle with the potential outcome of a situation then you are not in control of your thoughts and desires. You do not have a perspective on proper conduct and therefore cannot visualize the intended outcome of your dreams. Even if you do not know where you want to go but have a desire for change, you are already at some place along that path. Understanding and realizing where you are is the first step toward moving to a new understanding of where you think you might want to be. Once you have that aspect of your life under your own personal guidance you can readily seek assistance from others who will be sympathetic to your ideals. New opportunities will arise and you will be on your way again, until of course, you determine that that is not where you want to be either. Then you can redefine your desires and a new direction appears. The easy way out is usually that used by losers who blame others for their paltry existence and complain that they do not have the ability to make their own decisions because of self-proclaimed infringements. They will then use the excuse that they don't want to hurt anyone and so become self-denigrating martyrs. They can then deny themselves joy and pleasure while luxuriating in a miserable existence.

# 5

*Accept Pure Harmony in Your Mind and Body; If It Isn't There, Demand It of Yourself*

When trying to learn a new technique in any art form, especially one that takes into consideration the eventuality of creating or ending life as in a martial way, be sure that your vision isn't clouded by your viewpoint. Do not take the defeatist attitude of accepting a negative outcome in your life by suggesting to yourself that you are unable to accomplish something. It is with determination that you will attain your end result and the end result must be one of constant growth in, through, and as your personal ideal. This is how masters become masters and it is how they develop the need to continually invoke their own higher power to attain further levels of mastery. But, be aware that mastery consists of its own ascending reality. It is essential to understand your own motivation and thereby see into and through the actual accomplishment of your quest. There is never impossibility when it comes to personal accomplishment. There is, nonetheless, a desire to fail and be accepted by the vast majority of people who do nothing to enhance their own lives. Accepting pure harmony is an acknowledgment of having already attained that which you are working towards as already accomplished. It is an expression of your true self that reflects your soul.

# 6

## *If Advice Cannot Be Changed It Isn't Based in Reality Except for What You Tell Others*

We are all subject to the whims of our own fancy. We always take our own advice, good or bad, and act on it accordingly. When you ask someone for an opinion it is generally because you are seeking agreement with your own mind from another source. This is a good practice but only when you understand your own motives for asking others for advice. Ask yourself if the advice you are seeking is for your own benefit or is it for the benefit of flattering the person you are asking, or is it for the benefit of all concerned with yourself as the primary recipient of the good that it might bring? When someone presents you with an idea that can radically enhance your life, you should carefully, and with due consideration, think the message through rather than just haphazardly accepting it. That which you feel is substantive should be kept as is and appreciated. That which is open to contemplative position should be acknowledged and then put to practice in your universe if it suits your needs. When the information you get is not flexible, you should be most wary because it may have an external agenda that can dramatically deflect your own intentions. It goes without question that if certain matters are presented to you and they do not concur with your mindset they should be restructured if there is validity to their import, otherwise, they should be dismissed.

# 7

## *Things Too Easy to Get are Generally Too Hard to Keep*

It is not necessarily hard work that will get you what you desire. Rather, it is correct thinking about the value of your desires. Intensive thought and practice has to go into how you perceive your desires and what their true value is in your life. The mastery of an art comes with the constant devotion to the higher consciousness of the ideal represented by the mastery of that art. When the proper amount of effort and energy is put into something it becomes a part of person's being. When it is part of a person's being, it stays in place and continues to elevate the consciousness of the individual who puts the effort and energy into the attainment of mastery. If something is very simple to grasp it is, by nature, that much more difficult to maintain simply because of the perception of limited value accorded to gaining the objective. It is therefore not generally taken to be of much worth and the idea that it can be quickly reattained should it be lost becomes a grievous waste of time and energy. It is wise to contemplate the intended use of what you are trying to grasp before exerting effort to achieve what amounts to a Pyrrhic victory—one where victory costs much more than the value gained.

# 8

*A Person Who Truly Sees a Difference
in Things Sees Sameness in All Things*

What difference does it make if I use one style of a martial art and you use another style of a martial art? Nothing and no-thing. What difference does it make if I profess one way of thinking and you profess another way of thinking. If you are sincere and deeply thoughtful of your position, and maintain integrity, you will not become impressed with self-importance. Variations of approach to a personal desire for accomplishment may differ in application, but the intention of result is equal. Therefore, it is foolish to judge another and their work especially when I do not know the other person's intent. If I truly seek to understand my higher self, then I am too busy with my own endeavors instead of being concerned with yours. This creates harmony in one's sense of being. Where distinctions arise and another philosophy interferes with my striving for my own perfection, then conflict may ensue on whatever particular level. It is the person with the most resolve who will determine the outcome of the day and see through the foolish need for conflict and disharmony.

# 9

## *Focus on Principles, Not Politics*

We too often get involved with thinking incorrect thoughts because we are afraid of irritating those who might be of advantage to us. This is based on the idea that if you agree with someone, who is not in line with your own thinking for whatever reason, you will gain something that can help you reach your goals. This is not an intelligent way to think. When we subject our integrity to a lesser ideal than that which is in our heart and mind, we lose the perspective of being an individual and cause our self-esteem to be watered down in what eventually turns out to be a loss of morality and principle. Concurring with politics will not deflect the possibility of having to stand alone against the winds of change. Upon reflection we will always learn that when we donate our resolve to a lesser cause we are then without merit and can always be manipulated, especially if we have accepted praise or benefit from someone or something we do not a belief. Self-sustenance, though generally a harsh reality to live by, affords the strong person the resolve needed to maintain independence while enabling that resolve to act in accordance with the situation at hand.

# 10

*Too Many Books Cause Confusion
—Except for the Ones You Write*

How often do we find ourselves reading one version of something and then reading another version of the same thing in order to understand the original intent of our quest? With the exception of certain technical knowledge and having a fundamental idea of right and wrong, there is really nothing that has to be philosophically read, studied, or intellectually mused over once the decision to advance our personal ideal is determined. Though it is essential to know what works or doesn't work, depending on past experiences, it is best to draw a conclusion that you will understand through your own endeavors rather than the multitude of ideas that can be in conflict with each other. By knowing where you are,

you will generally know what to do (unless you are
oblivious to circumstance), and this is accomplished
by keeping one's mouth shut, paying attention to sur-
roundings, and absorbing while being absorbed.

Wed 07/11/2018          030 MM
                       POS: 3

------------------------------------------

(9780804850742)
THE WAY OF THE MODER    T $6.99

TAX                        $0.59
T O T A L               $7.58

CASH                       $8.00
CHANGE:                    $0.42

No. 373973    1 ITEM    TIME 11:07

------------------------------------------

You may return some unused items within
30 days with the original receipt.
Items must be in the original condition.
No returns or exchanges for the
following items: Special ordered items/
Sale items/Newspapers/Magazines/CDs&DVDs
/T-shirts/Comics/Travel guides/
Sundries/ etc.

POS: 3                    Wed 07/11/2018
033 MM

(9780804850742)
THE WAY OF THE MODER            $6.99 T

TAX                               $0.59
TOTAL                           $7.58

CASH                              $8.00
CHANGE:                           $0.42

No. 319973    1 ITEM    TIME 11:07

# 11

## *The Goods Men Derive From Conquest Drives Them Mad for More*

The weight of one's individual conquest is such that a conqueror most always thinks in terms of having to carry the assumed burden of conquest into the new territory being considered for accomplishment. The reality of this is that it causes confusion and frustration to run rampant especially when trying to rely on a past reputation for what may have only been valid at that previous time. How do you feel when you have accomplished something? There are any number of personal reflections you can experience. The one that is most predominant in the minds of most men is to accomplish more, and though it may seem easier to do more with less, the very nature of the accomplishment makes keeping out of your own way tiresome. For whatever reason you may think you have been successful, you are generally out of league with your own reality based on the idea that you may think you are the one who has accomplished this victory that requires a celebration. Actually, all that has happened is that a thought or two came into your mind, consciously or not; Heaven has aligned your experience to coincide with that thought. You haven't done a thing! But because you think you did, you are now going to further interfere with your profound abundance by determining which way circumstances should evolve that will cause you to create disturbances where none need exist. This mentality impedes universal progress as well as your own and truly slows you down. You can direct the universe but you cannot tell it how to get things done: strategy notwithstanding. It is all the Will of Heaven and, whether you like it or not, it feeds its own need, not yours.

# 12

*The Universe Knows What It Wants
You to Be and Do—and So Do You,
Which is Why You Reject It*

It is curious to find in one's life that paths unfold according to what you may think you wish to experience. Wishing is the problem and wishing is for children. When you wish upon a star it is usually the star that gets the wish granted. Determination of desire by focused thought is the only approach. However, consider the probability that the universe also directs you to that path for its own needs, which are impossible for you to determine. You did not invent yourself; regardless of your reasons for thinking you exist. This gives rise to the idea that Heaven moves in strange circles. Don't be concerned with the idea of success. It is a fallacy that few are able to understand because they continually brainwash themselves into thinking that financial remuneration is the end all and be all while trying to convince themselves that the true meaning of life is based on love. Love is a quaint notion that weak-minded people use as an excuse for the shortcomings in their lives. It can be an enormously powerful motivator when used correctly and for the benefit of all concerned, with you as the primary recipient of good. Do that and you will always have what you need, which will always be more than you could ever want—once you accept your greatness.

# 13

*Accept the Target's Acceptance*

This is not as confusing as it may appear on first reading. Think it through. What is the reason for a target's existence? A target exists in order to be hit when aimed at, or entirely destroyed. The reality is that if you approach what you consider to be a target, and you give it more authority in your mind than you should; you are giving it authority as well to maintain its existence. As a result, you do not have the commitment needed in order to overcome the adversarial aspect of it. You will be subjected to your own thinking in relation to the target, and will give it the very authority that you are trying to deny it. In order for a target to actualize itself and be destroyed in your experience, you must approach it with respect and integrity so that it will respect your approach and fulfill its destiny by succumbing to your intercourse with it, and by compliance, destroy itself.

# 14

*Take It*

When you want something, reach out and take it. When you are sincere in your desire to have something, it is a simple matter of accepting it into your life and doing so with utter ease and grace. This alleviates any and all stress or strain that may be preconceived as an aspect of attainment. Never try to wrest your success from others. It is basic nature for others to wish you well while simultaneously hoping for your failure. It is also the way of the world, except for the truly enlightened. Erroneous thinking based on outside influences leading to conflicts that are never necessary once the ideal of your desire is defined. Success falls into place when you earnestly desire it, and you must understand this freedom of choice in your acceptance. Otherwise, you will never ascend to your place of comfort, and confusion will result by your not knowing what it is that you want. Heaven knows what you want according to its own needs, but only according to your desire and acceptance that it grants to you. If you don't know what you want then you cannot expect Heaven to grant your desire even though it is being revealed to you time and again regardless of your own lack of acceptance. Think about what you truly desire, and when you are assured of your own mind, don't be amazed to see it unfold before you with hardly any effort on your part. It is yours for the taking.

# 15

*Clever People Have Little
Self-Esteem and So They Always
Look to Get Over on Someone*

Cleverness is detrimental to a warrior's conscience because of the need to fabricate situations in order to try and get over on an opponent. It is always best to be sincere in your dealings with others. When you have planned your attack, you will come to understand that cleverness is not something that can be relied upon in an ongoing confrontation. It can only assuage the naïve and childish. Mature warriors will not permit themselves to be cajoled by cute little tactics that are erroneously considered deceptive moves by an inadequately prepared adversary. People who try to defend their positions with ploys that usurp the true intention of the matter at hand will only find themselves to be readily destroyed when it comes time for redemption. It is precisely at this point that the clever person realizes that being unsubstantial does not hold water from overflowing the dam. They do not care for the benefit of all concerned but rather only for self-aggrandizement that eventually, not being grounded in substantive form, leaves them helpless and completely at the mercy of the astute. True accomplishment is based on determined focus—not baseless chatter. It is one thing to have desire and another thing, entirely, to create. When in life and death situations, and every conflict physical or mental is such, the person who wins will be the sincere devotee of winning by direct influence.

# 16

*Money is Not the Root of Evil but the Meaningless Things It Buys are Evil*

Look around you. How many of the possessions you have is actually doing something for you? Or is something there merely to impress others with what you purport to own? Curiously, it is the junk you keep for personal reasons that you are most inclined to protect when reality rings the bell. I am not speaking of art works of monetary value, though those too are usually an annoyance when you have to move quickly. Nor am I talking about objects that give you creature comfort, or the tools you use to perfect your personal discipline. When you consider the things that you own that have no intrinsic value, such as accumulations of things that you wonder about your need to keep, you will see that those are the very things that have distracted you from accomplishment of higher ideals. Things of value to you personally provide you with the inner strength necessary to maintain an ability to live with joy and freedom, but upon sincere reflection you will come to despise the entrapment of extraneous possessions that you have accumulated and will eventually want to rid yourself of them. Thinking that it is necessary to always acquire more "things," you overload your ability to appreciate the value of those things that truly empower you to ascend to higher levels of consciousness.

# 17

*Ease and Grace. Do It All With Ease and
Grace, Even That with Ease and Grace*

If you work hard, you are doing that. It doesn't mean
you will succeed. It does mean that if you do not realize
your goals in a relatively short time you will become
frustrated, confused, and probably cantankerous at the
same time. This is because you are trying to tell the universe what to do and you haven't truly defined what it
is that you want outside of a cursory and naïve desire
to ascend to someplace that you haven't fully acknowledged by contemplative definition. The easiest way to
attain perfection is to acknowledge it within you as
already accomplished. When you do that you will see
your entire desires manifest without your interference.
In the same way a samurai doesn't go out of his way to
try and impress the lord of his domain. He merely con-

tinues to practice until he and the art he does practice are the same at which time the lord will really know of the samurai's devotion. More so, the same with the power of Heaven. When you devote yourself to an accomplishment as already having been attained, you will see that you only need to refine your particular desires as you continue to elevate your mastery. Stress and strain in the guise of will power forces you to think you are very special and about what you desire. This happens to be the truth, but because you insist that the universe comply with your wishes, and not by your right of consciousness, things keep being delayed. Simply ascertain what you want to experience and begin living it. Mastery will come of its own accord when you practice your art and it will happen— with ease and grace.

# 18

## *Do Not Seek to Command; Seek to Teach. Do Not Seek to Obey; Seek to Understand*

No confusion here. Should the vagaries of life put you into situations where it is required that you issue orders compelling others to comply with your whim, be sure you have adequate resources to assure your directives. Giving orders is an aspect of great responsibility that has to do with more than material trinkets and weapons. It has to do with the lives of men. A wise leader will always see to it that what he is asking of his warriors is explained to them in such a manner that it leaves no room for doubt of success on their part. This is done through proper teaching of the ultimate goal, regardless of personal deception employed to get the work accomplished. Teaching intelligently will always cause the Will of Heaven to prevail. To blindly obey the directives of a leader indicates that you are not leadership material and will fall, if necessary without truly understanding what is at stake. When you know the meaning of a directive, even though you might not agree with the premise, your understanding of it will empower you with more capability to carry it out with more certainty of success. This will indicate to an astute governor that you are to be trusted and relied upon to fulfill the ultimate needs of the society. As a result, the role of commander will fall upon you and great good fortune will prevail in your life. It will give you inordinate authority when the time comes for you to rule.

# 19

## *Time Stands Still if You Go Fast Enough*

Many ancient apothegms and Zen postulates always sound as if they are cute riddles that cause one to laugh about their meaning such as the title for this section. This reasoning is always based on paradox, i.e., the obvious in reverse and not necessarily so. When you are thoroughly focused on the work you are doing, you will always find that time has a tendency to stop. Going fast enough means that you are not concerned with the actual speed of your artistic development, but rather with the outcome of your intended efforts. Consider works of art that are celebrated for their perfection that may have taken the artisan months, or perhaps years, to finish in perfect form. Consider the eternal now wherein all the planets and stars were made in less time than the snap of your fingers. There is hardly distraction when you are immersed in your work, if you are sincere in the level of accomplishment to be attained. Time only becomes relevant when you are thinking about doing something else rather than the task at hand that causes you to look at the clock. That is why masters are always seeking higher forms of expression and constantly meditate on the manner in which to accomplish it—they never think in terms of how long something will take to get done. When time stands still you no longer need concern yourself with bodily malfunctions. Your mind will continue to grow eternally and in turn your body will comply with the required functionality that houses the mind in proper fashion.

# 20

*Royalty Suggests Arrogance Until Overthrown by Humility; Then It Becomes Arrogance Again*

When ascending to higher levels of accomplishment and understanding about anything, including work or pleasure, you will always be able to overcome any obstacle; especially when you acknowledge your source as being a higher intelligence than you. In matters of men, regardless of their position, it is unfortunate that having once attained a certain amount of "fame," there is a tendency to become self-aggrandized even if it isn't outwardly demonstrated. This is dangerous and can cause you to lose control of what you may think is your self-ordained destiny. Maintaining humility is very difficult and only seems to work when you are struggling to get through the impediments that are life's challenges. Humility should never be expressed to anything less than Heaven. Whether you like it or not, Heaven is the only reason for your existence. Arrogance shown towards others when they are less fortunate than you is the first step to your demise…on any level, especially that of staying in the good graces of the Infinite. Enjoy your success, but realize that you are only as good as the last thing you have produced and you must never gloat about having done this or that when the reality is certain that you have only done your best work—in the future. Rely on your past experiences to propel you to further greatness and not bring a lethargy of your soul.

# 21

*Water Penetrates the Hardest Stone*
*as All Gives Way to Persistence*

Frustrations abound when you feel intuitively that you are on the correct path but are unable to surmount certain obstacles that seem to grow larger with every attempt to get over them. It is at this point that the courageous warrior will succeed if able to keep the desire for one's passion lit. Impediments are placed before us for whatever reason that we may conspire to believe but they are only indications of an inner need for ourselves to acknowledge our sincerity of and for accomplishment. What transpires in the human mind and breast is that we have been influenced by certain ideas that may not fit into our way of belief, but, possibly, well-meaning people who had no idea about their own inherent greatness have put them there. Eventually, the most difficult thing to accomplish gives in to persistence because of the very nature of the intensity and inquisitiveness of the seeker's desire. You may find it necessary to sit back for a while and try to learn about your internal obstacles that have nothing to do with the expression of your desire. This is called personal growth. "When the student is ready the master appears" is an old saw that does not necessarily hold water. Keep focused on your ideal and without qualm, accept it as already done. It will manifest in due form.

# 22

## *In Power and Quickness is Strength and Speed*

Strength and speed are the two things that will always impede a person's progress in any endeavor. Why? Because it is a method of measuring oneself against others and creates a false sense of competition. Competition may be good in certain aspects of being such as when it fosters creativity, but certainly not when the ultimate aim of the competition is to destroy a competitor. Behavior of that type is detrimental to the overall accomplishment of the deed regardless of the material gain and as a result it will never work as well as it should. There is no way to ascertain who is stronger or faster when everything is dependent on the actuality of the people involved and the perfection of their being at the time of measurement. You may have arisen in the

morning with irritable bowel syndrome and be con-
fronted with a mortal combat situation. In this situation your strength and speed are moot. Quickness
and power are completely different and of themselves
in that they enable a creator to focus without wor-
rying about what another aspect or condition may
imply. In this manner the strength and speed that is
required to attain a goal is protected and determined
by quickness and power. The true warrior, understanding this postulation will therefore become more
in tune with the universe and succeed with that much
more ease and grace.

# 23

## *In Times of Strife Wise Men May Use Evil With More Alacrity Than You Ever Could*

No one walks on water and cute little parlor tricks of walking on hot coals is really just a meaningless demonstration. People focused on their ideal never have to seek outside assistance (unless it is a specific need that must be addressed such as a technical issue). When the ideal is recognized for its value it is internalized into the mind of the seeker. If adversity presents itself and all sensible and logical means of creating harmony are futile, it may be time to get nasty. Because of the value of understanding integrity and virtue in a man's works, the use of dirty tricks may be relevant. This is not to be confused with cleverness, which has no substantive reality. Once the objective is accomplished and constituents are back in line with the objective of the progenitor, a return to normalcy is essential. Individuals who use evil ploys to maintain their positions can always realize that the experience has caused them to grow and they will overcome many shortcomings in the future via their own self acceptance.

# 24

## *Deeds are More Important Than Words, but Not to Poets*

Men can babble all they want and become slaves to their desires. This is not a good thing. It causes diversion from accomplishment and seeks to gain acceptance from the masses and individuals with whom a person may be directly involved. There are certain customs applicable to individual societies that must be adhered to or the entire fabric of that society will break down. For example, the taking of life may not be acceptable behavior in your society, but it may be acceptable in mine. On the other hand, if you are visiting a certain place where specific behavior is the accepted norm and you don't agree with it, then you should leave town or keep your distance from those practitioners of what you would consider a nefarious act. If your business includes dealing with those of an alien philosophy you would be wise to reconsider the reason for your continuing on in a relationship that bodes evil in your spirit. Coming to terms with it will ensure your success. That way you can go and come in perfect safety and without delay. Smart is better than intelligent—most of the time.

# 25

## *Appreciate Yourself or You Won't Be Appreciated*

This is the most essential attitude one can have relative to living a sane and prosperous life. Think about this most carefully. Who is more important than you? If you are not taking care of yourself to the extent that you want to take care of yourself, then how can you presume to take care of anyone or anything else except perhaps on a cursory level, which is at best a superficial mentality. There can be no one more important than you in the universe. There is no one more important than me in the universe. That is why I do not have difficulty in accepting you. Living thus, there is never a need for conflict. You have nothing that I really want that I cannot have for myself. If I think you can be of value to me and then I can proceed to celebrate my work and acknowledge you as having helped, and you will be that more happy with our relationship yet seeking to do more for the project that is given to us as a gift from Heaven. If I am greedy then you will withhold your beingness from me. I would prefer to have your gracious help and be able to say thank you with sincerity. It's most important to understand that what you are doing is merely an extension of the universe needing something done for reasons that you and I will never truly comprehend. Accepting this profound gift of life is an indication of thanks and should be treated with due respect and admiration for you having been given the responsibility of its earthly representation.

# 26

## *People With Nothing to Say Always Have Something to Say*

And that is why they can't be trusted. They are too busy trying to dissuade you from accomplishment because they themselves have nothing to do and with their problem of little self-esteem, they can do nothing productive for the benefit of all concerned; generally nothing of value for themselves. Avoid these people like the plague. The same goes for people with "attitudes." You know the kind I mean. Nose in the air; no one is good enough, etc. These people are psychologically insecure and will bully those who do not respond to them assertively. When you are concerned with your own welfare and your own work, you have no time for an attitude. You are generally too busy getting things done. What is even more destructive to your creativity is that in a situation where you take the advice of someone who is not completely sincere toward you, and having followed certain ideas they may have given you, they will always see to it that the reason for your success is that you heeded their advice. They will even go so far as to make you think that without them you would have never amounted to anything. Understand that you yourself are the progenitor of personal creativity and that with your perseverance and ardent desire to manifest a particular reality, you are the only one you should depend on. The output of your heart and soul should be your attitude. You should advise all others to take it on the arches.

# 27

*Never Choose Cheap Goods—*
*They are Much Too Costly*

If you cannot afford the best and you have an honest desire to be the foremost of your craft, regardless of whether you attain to it or not, then you certainly cannot afford the cheapest. It is wise to consider that the finest of materials and tools are produced for the ultimate ability of a craftsman to produce marvelous goods, and yes, it is possible to create something of value and worth without using the very finest of tools, but with them, and your subsequent mastery thereof, you are developing a synchrony with the creator of the tools to enhance your work as well. Everything is an aspect of everything else and nothing is total without complement. Again, especially when it comes to tools that you need to develop your craft. On the other hand, novices

and beginners should use materials that are not generally the costliest because if they do not continue in
their endeavor it is essentially a waste of materials.
When you learn that you have arrived at a discipline
that will give you pleasure as well as comfort in application of their nature, you have arrived at a point
where you and the tool are essentially the same thing.
At this point how dare you offend Heaven by not de-
manding of yourself to have the finest equipment that
is available? And curiously, the acquiring of such tools
is not relevant to cash outlay. Think about this.

# 28

## *The Heart is Essential If the Intellect is to Understand the Spirit*

Life consists of the body and the mind; together they comprise the soul. *Not* the body and the spirit. Spirit is a misunderstood term for those seeking ascension into the throne room of God. Because of the inevitability of defining what God may or may not be, there is a tendency to see It as a figment of imagination that enables someone to say that they alone are able to see into the mind of God. How silly. God is absolutely known to all men and all things in Its absolute and perfect form. It even has a name and will reveal that name to those who know how to ask. But that is another story. What you feel in your heart towards your work and to your world and to your universe is the passion that drives you forward. It induces the mind to come to terms with the variation of universal ideas and the development of the same as an aspect of the cosmos that you have defined for yourself. When you ascend to the level of utter consciousness with the creative parts of the universe you will readily find that you have already known that which is relatively unknowable and be able to live according to your desire through your concept of yourself. That aspect of your being is the true soul and can only be understood when you give yourself over to the forces that compel you to do the work you think you have chosen for yourself. Only then will you come to understand that you and the spirit of what it is that you are involved with are the same exact thing. There is no need to differentiate between the body and the mind as they make up the spirit of life. *That* is your soul.

# 29

## *It is Easier to Understand the Difficult Than the Simple*

When something is presented as a difficult problem the seeker should ascertain the correct understanding of the problem in order to solve it. Generally, there is only one answer and so the quest becomes simple: "A" must be considered as "A" and this is the definitiveness you must seek. To understand this is to realize that the universe reveals all that is necessary for comprehension of any riddle when the situation is queried in the correct manner. The right question always includes the answer being sought after. Accepting the hidden simplicity of a quest is the root of true genius and that is the nature and mystery of perplexity. On the other hand, when something appears simple, too many variations of the same answer can exist that will break down the cogency of functional usage. It becomes matters of opinion and therefore loses relevancy to the overall needs of the individual or the society that seeks the answer. In combat you either "kill" the enemy directly or discuss the need to provide for his family. That is how you determine your own life or death.

# 30

*Humble Opinions are Based on Not Knowing What You are Talking About*

This is my opinion—and it is certainly not humble. When you have studied something for a good deal of time, and you have essentially come to understand the mutual relationship between yourself and your art, you have essentially become one and the same thing. Why should you try to impress those who may not have any idea about what you are talking about with false modesty? Doing so will only cause you to eventually question your own morality and force you to become subservient to your own ideal. You may want to show someone the why and wherefore of a certain technique, perhaps, but never permit your self to actualize your self through personal abasement as a direct expression of the spirit of the craft you desire to master. Such irresolute thinking and behavior will eventually turn your greatness into mediocrity because of an internally developed disbelief in your own reality. When you seek to make excuses for yourself in order to alleviate the fears of the masses all you are doing is trying to come down to their level, which will cause you to stop thinking highly of the craft that the creative force has provided for you. True humility and humbleness should only be offered to Heaven, and the form of that should be of utter mastery.

# 31

## *To Perish Quickly Think Only of Yourself*

Thinking only of yourself is sometimes a good thing but only when you are considering the value of yourself to others. Thinking only of yourself can assist you in developing the necessary persona and skills you need to construct a viable and healthy life without becoming arrogant, conceited, and filled with false pride. Unfortunately, most people have a tendency to forget that they are part of an all-encompassing universe that relies on each part of itself to amplify itself. I think only of myself when I am trying to learn another way of delivering my message to whoever wants to hear it. As good as it may appear to be, it becomes negative if I am impressed with my own self-worth and cannot do that which is required of me to be of value to others. It is not beneficial to others when I think only of the returns I will get from my efforts and only consider giving it to the world when I am assured they will respond in kind— or with deprecating gifts. Think only of yourself, yes, but do it for the benefit of all concerned.

# 32

## *Education Should Never Be Confused With Learning*

The best way to get a message across is through education. It has always been so. Problems arise when one group tries to instill its thoughts upon another and doesn't explain the validity and intention of the new message to the target society, and so mandates are issued. People will react against sudden intrusions in their lives and have to be hard pressed to follow the new order of things. When a group has no option but to comply under the threat of more difficult hardships they should seek to learn about the methods being used and the message being delivered. When this is understood it is easy to overturn the aggression being foisted upon them. If education is not used as a tool for enlightenment and ignorance prevails, then abject hatred will follow and turmoil will reign until it explodes into outright rebellion. When trying to control others with your will it is best to make them think the new regime is their own idea and will be of great benefit to them as well. When education is appropriately handled and dealt with, armed conflict can generally be avoided.

# 33

*Be Good to Yourself First and Then Worry About the Rest of the World*

How often do we think we should do everything for everyone else even though we know it is injurious to our own well-being? Too often, more than likely, and it is based on the idea that acceptance by others will make our own lives sweeter. This is not so. If you satisfy your own needs first and have fairly much all of what you want you have no problem giving with a full heart to others. If giving is not done in this manner then things will be given grudgingly regardless of the best intentions and will reflect in the actual gift. "Things" have the propensity for carrying the attitude of the deliverer. The same mentality applies when giving gifts. Do you give a gift with your full sincerity, or do you give a gift as a cursory gesture to alleviate an obligation? When you give a gift to someone it should be based on the idea that this particular thing is something that you would enjoy for yourself as well. Your attitude will reflect in the giving and the person receiving your gift unless they are callous and have no sensibility about being human will show true appreciation.

# 34

## *If You Can't Do It Right, You Can't Do It Wrong*

Trying to do something without proper planning and forethought will generally lead you into the abyss of not getting anything done at all. Though things may appear to be completed you will always wonder as to whether or not you actually did the job properly. If you don't think about the potential outcome of your accomplishments then you were probably not in harmony with the needs of the project and the results will be plain enough. Think through your actions before you apply them as deeds. You might find an easier way to accomplish something and really be of value to humanity. When things are done through the belief that we are immortal and can do anything at any time, we usually find that someone else is trying to accomplish the same thing and we are caused to think that possibly the other person is doing a better job. We will then try to find shortcuts to our own accomplishment. This brings about folly and the attendant frustration about trying to figure out why something that you thought so simple to do didn't work according to your whim.

# 35

*If You're Gonna Play, Play—Don't Play*

This is a bit of a play on words here but the message should be very obvious. When practicing your craft, it is essential that you do not permit lackadaisical attitudes to prevail under any circumstances. Ambivalence regarding your work shows up in ways that you cannot be aware of or foresee. When you have decided that the reality of your art is indeed your mastery of it, you will have no choice but to work at it with total resolve. You will find the joy and pleasure of your project and will share the enthusiasm for greatness that reflected in the work and through the work. When you define the "work" you are doing and accept it as accomplished in relative perfection, you as the artist, regardless of the definition of the project, will become one with it and both you and the project will ascend in acceptance by those observing. Otherwise, what you are doing is for an ulterior motive and the inner core of the art itself will deny you safety, comfort, and revelation.

# 36

## *Politeness is Not a Sign of Weakness*

We live in times that are essentially the same as any other time in history with the exception of the shrinking globe, the modernity of technology, and the availability of immediate communications via the internet. Other than that there is hardly anything different within any society. The result of this makes it essential that we come to understand each other and to respect cultural differences. It is a sad thing that our lack of mutual respect for one another is creating more and more dissension among people. As a result, less and less civility is being taught to children, (perhaps the elderly might make the effort to educate the young). For the most part, and it is very obvious, parents themselves do not have the information turned to knowledge that is required to properly guide their young. This results in a diffident approach to relations with everyone for the most part by everyone. Politeness, i.e., "thank you," "please," "excuse me," etc., have become naïve notions that current society would have you think is a sign of weakness. That is the paradox of its own weakness. In the samurai world, essentially the world of bushido, politeness was an absolute requisite to maintain order within the various segments. It also denoted self-respect based on self-esteem. And it worked very well even as the precursor to slaying your enemy.

# 37

*Humility is Sometimes a Very Necessary Thing—Especially When You're Outnumbered*

How many times do we find that reality raises it's ugly head most especially when you are unprepared? When a warrior keeps his or her own vision uncontaminated, only success will prevail, whereby firm concentration creates a clear path to be followed. Should you put yourself in harm's way for any reason, it is usually because you are unaware of the non-productive thoughts that will create disharmony in such form. The same applies even more so to a combat situation where the odds are simply too overwhelming to deal with. There is nothing wrong with having to back off when this happens and thereby permit yourself to better prepare for the next encounter where you can lessen the opposing odds in your favor and readily deal the blows required for total victory. Humility is never to be construed as opposite to a strong ego, but rather that it enhances the ego by permitting you to return to that same victory and usually live to talk about it.

# 38

*Understand the Similarities
of Fate and Free Will*

Many men and women believe that they make the choices in their lives according to their own whim. Others have no doubt that they are the plaything of some higher intelligence and that there is nothing they can do to change the course of their lives. Both ideas are, of course, right, though based on individual perception. Equally, both ideas are wrong. You only make choices based on the self-aggrandizement of your illusions. As you are evolved from the necessity of Heaven, this reality lends itself most fortuitously to the true statement that there is no such thing as yin and yang, which is not to suggest that yin and yang do not exist. Does the universe create for you specifically, or do you have to tell it what to do? Interesting that you don't accept both realities. If you did then you would find the simplicity of it all in that what you take for granted is a supposition and that it is all the truth you need to know.

# 39

*There is No Such Thing as Yin and Yang, Which is Not to Suggest That Yin and Yang Do Not Exist*

When a man decides that one thing is better than another, distinction is being forced into a situation that may not be of value to anyone. To think that one thing can be better than another limits your ability to understand all that is comprised of the complete matter. This is right, that is wrong; this is good, that is bad. If you force your intentions on others and they are of a different mentality than yours is, you are essentially creating a conflict that may only be rectified by conflict. It is always best to consider the particular needs of another person and see the possibility of working in harmony for the benefit of all concerned. Compromise is not a bad thing when it is used to accomplish a greater good. Yin and yang also suggests preconceived notions about the way things are supposed to be according to your own self. Others may simply not be in agreement with you. It is not wise to put yourself into situations that can get you killed for a meaningless reason. It is much easier to live your life through your work, which may also be a fantasy, but at least it is yours.

# 40

*Deceptive Technique Should
Be Avoided Whenever Possible*

It is always best to be sincere in your dealings with others. People tend to become very defensive when they are put into circumstances where they think they are losing control of a situation. People who fear the ascension of their own beingness through continued learning are to be avoided unless they particularly seek you out as a teacher, but that is another matter. Deception is detrimental to a warrior's conscience because of the need to fabricate situations in order to try and get over on an opponent. In matters of commerce this may be acceptable as a ploy to confuse matters for the sake of appearance, however, in the final analysis, especially in physical confrontation, deception will only temporarily give you a presumptive advantage. When in life and death situations, and every conflict physical or mental is as such, the person who wins will be the sincere devotee of winning by direct influence. It is best to practice your craft with the intention of overcoming shortsightedness. Do not allow your view to confuse your vision.

# 41

*Hoping is Based on Non-Acceptance;*
*Wishful Thinking is Willful Denial*

Life is best enjoyed when you accept your gifts from Heaven without questions. What you receive in life is usually what you actually need but because you tend to think in terms of what others have, you get yourself into a position of envy that will limit your ability to ascend to a higher level of accomplishment. Then, you begin to "hope" that things will eventually get better. The truth is that things are always growing and expanding in the universe, but you are not accepting them as such. If you will determine for yourself what it is that you want to experience, you will find that it is already in place, and that all you have to do is believe that it is yours by knowing it as real and living it as real. Then of course, comes "wishing" and that is a total waste of time because it suggests that you are not believing you deserve something and are therefore, by the wishing itself, denying its appearance in your life. It is best to accept yourself according to the dictates of your true self and not what others tell you is important for you to do. Wishing an enemy dead is one thing; making him dead is a completely different matter.

# 42

*You Only Know Love If You Know Hate. It is Best to Know Neither, but Simply to Be*

Being judgmental is a quick way to lose perspective on anyone you deal with as well as anything you would attempt to master. Before you can truly appreciate your own intentions it is wise to think about the entire matter from both sides and see if it is honestly what you want to experience. To instantly love someone, or to instantly hate, will give you tremendous unrest and create anxiety in all of your affairs. As difficult it may seem to be, to not evaluate any condition unless it is specifically detrimental to you would be to judge something that has deceptive appearances. This attitude based on your personal fears and inadequacies rather than accepting the situation for what it is, and then seeing where it can be used to your own advantage. Should you find that you love something, then by all means do everything you can to enhance the life of that love. If you decide that you do not want to be involved with a situation then simply walk away from it remembering that you are not all that important that you would have to destroy its beingness with any weak minded thoughts. Accept things at face value and, if they are pleasing to you, enjoy them. If they are not, don't waste your precious time trying to alleviate a bad situation. It will only make things worse—for both of you.

# 43

## *Do What You Tell Yourself to Do and Don't Take No for an Answer*

How many times have you come to the conclusion that what you want to pursue is the right and only course of action for you to take? Many times no doubt, and if you are a thinking person, you have spent a good deal of energy in arriving at the point of decision; you have weighed all of the good aspects against the bad aspects and have prepared the path you will now embark upon. Being of resolute mind you start the work but for whatever reason an immediate block to the accomplishment of your endeavor appears. This can be anything: another person in your life, a lack of finances, fear of being unable to do what you told yourself you wanted to do, and worst of all, a lack of belief in yourself. When your inner thoughts begin to nag at you and tell you that you are not really adequate for the job you have set before yourself, it is exactly at this moment that you must take a firm hold of your mind and demand that Heaven assist you in this accomplishment. Not to do so will cause a pattern of failure to be born and the result will be a lack of confidence in anything further that you do based on the ideas you are giving yourself about being unworthy to accomplish your goals. When you want something done, regardless of appearances, demand that your soul comply.

# 44

## *People Will Believe in Anything That Works Even When It Doesn't*

There is always a tendency to want to believe that something will be good for us based on its appearance. The result is that most people put too much value on the outer aspect of the matter and do not consider the internal function. Desire will do for you what you truly need to have done. This is the difference between needing and wanting; the former, for some reason is always there and made available to and for you; the latter is what causes all the consternation in our lives because it simply may not be viable for personal attainment. If you are presented with a very flashy sword and scabbard you will generally have a tendency to think that the finery that appears before your eyes is what will do the job for you when a job needs to be done. How foolish it is to think that the appearance of something will presuppose the practice needed to master its reality as well as your own. Believing in something based on appearance will always cause you to relinquish the effort required to make it work according to its external design and can further, by your own misguided ego aggrandizement, force you to waste countless hours on something that does nothing to enhance the quality of your life.

# 45

## Don't Consider the Rewards of Your Work and the Results Will Be Better

When a man strives to be rewarded before he has accomplished something he will always find that his path is strewn with debris of his own incorrect thinking. This will cause him to manifest something that has no intrinsic worth. It is wise to consider that the work is always more important than the worker until the worker has come to terms with the true intent and purpose of the project he is considering. The needs of the project will always dictate what has to be done. Ignoring this aspect will cause weakness of mind and intention to come forth and the end result will be shoddy at best. When perfection is sought after, even though completeness of perfection itself cannot be expressed on the plane of existence we inhabit, it is incumbent upon us to seek after it and watch as the efforts of our labors take on a life of its own. This expresses the will and perfection of Heaven more than the limited ideas we think we understand. When a man has come to understand and to appreciate what has been accomplished for the pleasure of Heaven, he will find that he becomes one with the work and at that point he is enlightened.

# 46

## *To Be One Thing, You Must Also Be the Opposite*

How can anyone expect to be balanced in mind and fair in meting out justice when required if understanding both sides of the matter is not an aspect of consideration? This is why judges are often ridiculed based on their political intent that refuses to acknowledge the simplicity of resolution; being swayed this way or that according to the dictates of the people they are by necessity required to assuage. The ancients have told us, over and again, that this is the easiest way to determine the just outcome of any situation. Have the conditions of concern brought before you by impartial persons who will only tell you the facts of the matter and not the names and places of the event. In this manner you will be certain to arrive at an honorable and just conclusion if you are sincere in your endeavor to mete out the appropriate decision without partiality. Regardless, you will still find that you have offended someone who might often be a close ally or friend. If being of less sterner stuff, you would be wise to not be put into situations that will cause you to foster enemies. You will do that, regardless of your endeavors, anyway.

# 47

## *Greatness Spreads Its Wealth Without Restriction Except to You, Right?*

In matters of daily commerce you will always strive, if your endeavor is focused then you will glean as much as possible from the efforts of your labors. When you have put much sincerity and integrity in your work and you know that you are entitled to a fair compensation, you will still have a tendency to think that you are selling yourself short and not getting your just rewards. How do you arrive at this conclusion? You try to equate what you are doing with the works of others. This leads to frustration and then lends itself to producing works that are inadequate to the ideal you have set before you. Artists and businessmen must believe that their output can always be better and will endeavor to get as much reward as possible. This is a natural state of mind. The difficulty arises when you think that others, whom you judge to be less functional, mentally and spiritually according to your inclination, get more of a reward than you think they deserve. This causes envy and presupposes greed that will interfere with the true worth of the work that has been assigned to us by Heaven through whatever venues. And it all comes from Heaven. Rewards are meted out according to the true value of what we are creating. You will always get what you deserve irrespective of what you think you are entitled to and that is based on your preconceived ideas of your true worth and value.

# 48

*Heaven is Obedient to All Things.*
*If That Isn't True, Then You Aren't Here*

It is required that you understand yourself in relation to the universe, without which you would simply not exist. This is a fundamental idea that exists because you are able to think, but before you came into existence there had to be some sort of energy that permitted your life to unfold, regardless of how you pursue your desires. To consider that there is no creative force is to become nihilistic and without purpose. It does not matter that you do "things" that you may consider relevant. The plain fact of truth is that without your mind you do not have the wherewithal to even presume to conceive of an idea. Once you acknowledge a higher form of intelligence than that which you think you have, you will quickly see the futility of non-existence and seek to do more for your fellow man but only when you are able to realize that you are the primary recipient of all the good in the universe that is given to you to share. You do this because you know that the more you give the more you will have to give. Heaven gives the thoughts you generate in your mind to you as well. It does not matter to the source of all things that you believe this or not.

# 49

## *Be Sure You're Right and Then Proceed, Even if You're Wrong*

Once you have determined a course for your actions it is essential that you proceed to develop them to the highest level of perfection that you can attain. Regardless, there will be times that you will pursue something and eventually come to see it as false and will need a change in consciousness to afford you the pleasure of living a sane and productive life. When people think that whatever they do, right or wrong according to their own dictates, they usually end up in a morass of difficulty when trying to live their lives in accordance with their highest expectations. The only way to know if what you have chosen to do is correct for you, is to experience it on a mentally awake level. If it still impels you forward, stay with it and it will reveal its essence. Then you can make the proper choice of continuing or stopping. If you have chosen the right path, few if any impediments will occur. If there are too many impediments, you have chosen the wrong path. On the other hand, if things are coming together with too much ease, as if you don't even have to pursue it, then you can be assured that either you are extremely blessed or are oblivious to your impending doom.

# 50

## *Give Life and Death to All Things but Don't Seek to Own Them*

Things that are created in and through your mind are the things that define you to yourself. Still, it does not matter what your thoughts are on the matter. All is given by Heaven and therefore they may be considered to be on loan. If they are given to you and you begin to work through them and come to understand the reality of your gifts, then it is foolish to hoard the gift for yourself. It will end up having no meaning to you or to anyone. The same is for the very rich man who does not use his wealth for the enjoyment of his life; he deprives himself of pleasure thinking that if he indulges in anything he will be giving it away. The exact opposite is true. When you have finished with something that has or has not given you pleasure in the past it can be considered a form of death of a past experience. Let it go; it is no longer yours. Life will reveal to you new experiences and the same thinking should apply in your newness as well. To understand this with more certitude, keep in mind that when you die, you go out by yourself, ego notwithstanding.

# 51

*Endeavor to Come to Terms With the Tragedy of Your Own Inconsequence*

When a man comes to truly understand that all accomplished things originated from someone or something prior to his involvement he will also come to see that without the very ideas that preceded him he would be hard pressed to create anything. Ideas come to the person who constantly enhances his vision based on the thoughts in his imagination of his desires and dreams. Those thoughts are put there by something and if they are disregarded then nothing will come of it. More than likely the idea will be put into another mind, and so it goes until the idea germinates and manifests into physical reality. To have thought of a device that would illuminate a dark room is simply a flight of fancy. True genius comes to bear when a man does not permit the thought to be released back to the nothingness from where it came. Persistence breeds causality and the notion that the fulfillment of one's desire is manifested only by the higher intelligence of the universe—with you or without you.

# 52

## *When You See a Man in All of His Glory Know That He has Known, or Will Know Shame*

Until a person is able to realize their true worth in the universe and not in their particularly small sphere of influence, all forms of anxiety can cause diversion from acceptance of the perfect ideal. This anxiety causes clever tricks and ploys to be used to overcome all the times of doubt and pain without true resolve of the matter at hand. At this point the person is incapable of reaching the goal desired and becomes further mired with confusion and frustration. It is at that time that release of ego's restrictive conditions become essential for survival. It is also when a man comes to understand his relevance and acknowledges his blessings in whatever form and reality of the desire he wants manifested. Not to do so will cause him to remain captive to arrogance, conceit, and false pride that will eventually bring him down.

# 53

*Say "Thank You," Even
When You Mean It*

It is never good to be superficial in your acknowledgment of anything. Doing so keeps you from fully ap-
preciating what you are trying to accomplish and others
will readily see that you are being insincere. They will
react in ways that can eventually bring difficulty into
your life. When thanking someone or something, true
enthusiasm is best expressed when the words you use
convey the spirit of your intention, which should always be on the same level you would expect for yourself.
Lack of conviction in your thankfulness of anything
will cause you to begin thinking in terms of mediocrity.
When you are thankful for something and mention that

you are, especially to another, do so with an acceptance of your greater good regardless of who might be doing their work on your behalf or for their own needs. Never grudgingly give thanks for anything.

# 54

## *Conquering Your Fears is the Only Victory Worth Having —So is Conquering Your Joys*

Most of us have been taught from the earliest days of our childhood that we should always face with courage the hardships that come along at various times in our lives. Though this may seem to be an adequate lesson learned from our parents or others, it is not always as simple as it seems, especially when we have started to grow and are faced with the inconsistencies of the world. Many will try to overcome their supposed inadequacies by partaking in foolish behavior and getting into one difficulty after another. This generally continues on throughout life unless it is halted in one's own minds. Never permit yourself to think that you are incapable of accomplishing anything that you want to experience. When you are faced with a frightening situation it is at that very moment that you must insist upon not giving what is frightening to you authority to control any aspect of your life. The same applies to what may appear to be an overwhelming joy. It is this same joy that could lead you into a sense of false security and cause you to lose mastery of yourself. Treat those things that are frightening and those that are joyous as extensions of your life experience that you determine for yourself as having no power to cause disturbance or false humility.

# 55

*Good Fortune can Be Quelled by Bad Behavior Even Though Bad Behavior is Sometimes Virtuous*

You will find in life that there are times when you think you are in complete control of the world and venture forth to prove it by the most inane and superficial methods. You think because you are sharing in a profound success that you are immune to any causation that can put a stop to your ventures. This is foolish and dangerous action and thinking. The reverse is where you want to accomplish something that you truly believe is for the benefit of everyone in your life and take it into your hands to make things happen for them in your determination to be a leader. It is essential in this mentality that you are fully aware of the needs of all concerned and are willing to take the risk of creating your own downfall should failure ensue. When you do this and you do it with utter resolve Heaven will see your sincerity and bring forth that which you want to experience. In all matters, it is also essential that you are aware of the source of all good and pay ultimate homage towards it.

# About the Author

Stephen F. Kaufman is the author of the world-wide, best-selling interpretations of *Musashi's Book of Five Rings*, *Sun Tzu's Art of War*, and *Shogun's Scroll*. He has also written *The Living Tao, Zen and the Art of Stickfighting, Sword in the Boardroom,* et al. His books, selling in the hundreds of thousands, are acclaimed by many as the finest interpretations of classics and contemporary teachings to date and are considered essential reading for groups and organizations interested in progressive managerial and motivational strategy development via life enhancement skills.

Hanshi Kaufman is the founder of Self-Revealization Acceptance,™ the world's most advanced reality facilitation and motivation concept first introduced in 1993. His books, *Self-Revealization Acceptance* and *Practicing Self-Revealization Acceptance* have become classics in the field.

Acknowledged as a true founding father of American karate, he was elected to the title and rank of Hanshi, 10th Dan, the most prestigious accomplishment in the martial arts world in 1991 by international peer associations. His martial arts system, Hebi-ryu, School of the Snake, is recognized as one of the most realistic martialist methods in the world. A career spanning close to 60 years starting on Okinawa in the 1950's includes teaching and practical experience with the U. S. Air Force, law enforcement agencies, NYC Board of Education, NYC Dept. for the Aging, litigation firms, marketing groups, corporations, community centers, and private schools.

Hanshi lives in New York City and spends his time traveling, teaching, writing, and producing his cable television show, Hanshi's World™. His seminars are tailored for any audience or strategic situational objectives. An authority on management and motivation training and development, Hanshi empowers audiences to turn every challenge: business, military, and personal, into an opportunity by demonstrating definitive working techniques guaranteed to bring about advantageous results *"for the benefit of all concerned."*

For more about Hanshi, visit www.hanshi.com for book descriptions.
Contact Hanshi by email: sfk422@gmail.com
Author blog: hanshibooks.wordpress.com
Facebook: @hanshikaufman